WHY POP MUSIC SUCKS

THE MAKING OF THE POST ROCK N ROLL ERA

JERRY BAIDEN

JETLAUNCH

Copyright © 2024 by Jerry Baiden

All rights reserved.

No portion of this book may be reproduced in any form without written permission from the publisher or author, except as permitted by U.S. copyright law.

This publication is designed to provide accurate and authoritative information in regard to the subject matter covered. While the publisher and author have used their best efforts in preparing this book, they make no representations or warranties with respect to the accuracy or completeness of the contents of this book and specifically disclaim any implied warranties of merchantability or fitness for a particular purpose. Neither the publisher nor the author shall be liable for any loss of profit or any other commercial damages, including but not limited to special, incidental, consequential, personal, or other damages.

Printed in the United States of America

First Printing

Book Cover by Jerry Baiden and JETLAUNCH

Orders by U.S. trade bookstores and wholesalers. Cataloging-in-Publication Data Baiden, Jerry.

Why Pop Music Sucks: The Making of the Post-Rock N Roll Era / Jerry Baiden. p. cm.

ISBN: 979-8-89079-122-1 (Paperback)
ISBN: 979-8-89079-123-8 (Hardback)
ISBN: 979-8-89079-124-5 (Ebook)

Contents

Introduction v

Chapter One 1
THE 1980s: THE BEGINNING AND THE END

Chapter Two 8
THE 1950s: THE BIRTH OF ROCK AND ROLL

Chapter Three 16
THE 1960s: POP MUSIC COLLEGE

Chapter Four 21
THE 1970s: "I HAVE ALWAYS IMAGINED THAT PARADISE WILL BE A KIND OF 1970s"

Chapter Five 26
THE 1990s: THE 1996 TELECOMMUNICATIONS ACT KILLED THE RADIO STAR

Chapter Six 31
THE 2000s: THE SERPENT AND ITS FRUIT OF CHOICE

Chapter Seven 37
THE 2010s: TECHNOLOGICAL MIS-ADVANTAGES

Chapter Eight..............................42
THE 2020s: GOING FORWARD?

Chapter Nine..............................53
ANECDOTAGE

Chapter Ten...............................67
SPECIAL ADDITIONAL CHAPTER

Glossary..................................75

Bibliography..............................91

Index.....................................97

Introduction

This book is not meant to be an overview of the artists of the time. There are already many existing books, podcasts, videos, etc., on that subject. Neither is it meant to be a history of pop music. Again, there are hundreds of books, videos and documentaries on the history of Rock N Roll, R&B, Pop, Classical, Folk, Country, Jazz, etc. The scope of this book is about the slow, nonstop, yet fantastical progression of socioeconomic events that led to where pop music is now.

For musicians and "seasoned industry folk:" Let us commiserate. Been thinking that modern pop music sucks? You're right about that, and there are good reasons for why it does. Why Pop Music Sucks will be our guide.

For middle-school, high-school, and college students: Do you ever feel that life is only about going to school so you eventually make enough money to live? Why Pop Music Sucks will help you understand that issue in less than 100 pages, with pop music front and center.

For educators: Musical illiteracy is epidemic among young students in general where they are unaware of previous forms and iterations of pop music. Why Pop Music Sucks will help your students understand what occurred to create what they have now, and in less than 100 pages.

Chapter One
The 1980s
The Beginning and the End

The 1980s transitioned Americans from analog at the beginning of the decade to digital at the other end. Before this decade, households were all analog, nothing was digital, and all we had was a TV, a radio, a record player, a cassette player, and a phone. Life in the 80s, however, was buzzing with the excitement of new ways to navigate the world. The first major event was cable TV, which entered our homes in approximately 1980. Cable TV had been in the works for many years, and made itself a common household presence very quickly. One positive outcome was that we no longer had to go up on the roof and risk our lives to install a TV antenna or two. Instead, a technician would come to your home and install the cable system themselves. This was the beginning of an important element of our lives. Subscribers were easy to obtain, and it was cheap, of course, at least at first.

Music Television (MTV) launched in August of 1981. It was a 24/7 video channel that broadcast and rotated a small number of music videos around the clock because of the relative scarcity of existing music videos at the time. However, that changed things for pop music overnight. In fact, MTV changed the entire music industry overnight. <u>Any</u> band or artist featured on MTV became an overnight superstar, and subsequently, MTV became the most powerful, media source/network for pop music for the next 30-plus years. *Everyone* was watching this channel. I was watching MTV at all hours of the day and night, even though I had seen the current videos numerous times already.

In 1983, Nintendo released its first game console in the U.S., and video games were introduced to the masses around the globe. Video games were already vigorously in the making in the 70's, but it was the 80s when they became a common household item. From there, video gaming became something in which all kids were going to involve themselves with, especially boys. Unfortunately for pop music, gaming was going to be the main activity for young folks going forward, rather than musical instruments. Thus, video games became a huge "nail in the coffin" of traditional pop music.

In 1984, Michael Jackson produced a video featuring the title song from his album *Thriller*, which was one of the best-selling albums of all time. He made the video into a mini-musical with the help of director John Landis.

The structure of the video:

- Intro with no music. The story is being set-up.
- The song begins.
- The song ends, but the video does not.
- This transitions into a choreographed dance section with Michael and his friends made-up as zombies.

The "Thriller" video was awesome and revolutionary. Prior to this video, music videos consisted of a band or artist lip-synching the song in a studio setting. However, Michael was not going to settle for that. From that point on, he showed us a spectacular way to create videos, and little has changed for music videos since then. Currently (2024), most videos feature the first three points of Jackson's video structure but without a choreographed dance section.

The attraction of this visual and theatrical spectacle created a more visual-dance perspective and approach for the industry. In fact, this video concept would affect live performance as well. Subsequently, when Michael and other artists like Madonna went on tour, these new elements exerted financial pressure for those artists. The hiring of dancers, videographers, and more technical staff was a boon for these newly added crew members. However, artists such as Jackson had to feed them all, put them up somewhere on the road, and transport all of them from show to show. These issues were a primary reason why ticket prices rose steeply from the time of that video onward.

Understand here that choreographed dancing can "enhance" a musical performance, but why would it be necessary? This question is more rhetorical than literal, because its answers are difficult to prove and are theoretical in nature:

1) Music videos have created an expectation of extraneous elements that accompany a singular music piece or song.
2) Viewers/listeners' attention spans are somewhat shorter now (I am being very generous here). Further, the level of focus and what they are focusing on has changed greatly over time.
3) Music artists cannot "stand on their own." Can a singer or a band get up on a stage and simply perform a set only by expressing themselves musically?
4) The amount of money generated by a major music production is crazy. Everybody wants a piece of it, especially newly added crew members who did not have a place at the table before.

I saw Whitney Houston on her very first tour at the Warfield Theater in San Francisco. I still have the ticket stub. Whitney was the opening act for Jeffrey Osborne, who was riding high on his big hit, "Stay With Me Tonight." Whitney was just getting started with her first single, "You Give Good Love." At that time, visual bells and whistles were neither expected nor needed.

I would assume that dancers and video would have been very distracting to us at the time, particularly when you have a singer who could stand on stage and sing a grocery list and have it be the most beautiful grocery list that you had ever heard in your life. So, let us take into consideration the term "distract," which means to draw or direct someone's attention to a different object, thing, or whatever—to divert. Therefore, why would any music artist use other media elements that could possibly distract or divert attention from themselves? While it can be an enhancement of some sort, but it can also distract and divert.

In 1986, the CD (Compact Disc) made an abrupt arrival onto the scene. Yours truly was the "jazz buyer" at Tower Records in Mountain View, California at that time. I had to change the bins that had contained LPs (Long Play vinyl records) from the beginning of time and adapt them to CD packaging. The industry did think about the issue of retail product bins and devised a packaging system in which two packaged CDs would occupy the same space as a double LP album. The CD, this Sony invention, changed everything yet again. A CD's capacity was approximately 78 minutes of audio as opposed to an LP at around 40 minutes, and its fidelity was quite consistent and user-friendly. While you had to be very careful in setting up a record turntable, CD players did not have that problem. In addition, you could throw the CD down a cliff and probably still play it after retrieving it at the bottom, which also made it a very complimentary format for playing music in cars. The CD signaled a major change from the LP going forward. For whatever it accomplished, the CD was the end of the everyday use of the vinyl LP and the beginning of everyday use of whatever digital formats followed.

With its expanded capacity, CDs were a larger canvas for artists and their excesses, which inevitably would result sometimes in "watering-down" of an artist's work. When you have a smaller "canvas," you must be much more strategic in your choices for what actually gets on that canvas. Only your best material goes on that LP. However, with a 78-minute CD, not only does your best material make it onto the CD, but you could also include a demo track, a live track or two, and a hidden track… and maybe even an interview.

The LP was still king for a while (2 more years) until CD sales surpassed LP sales. LPs were approximately $10 at the time, while CDs were around $16. At that point, LPs cost around $4.00 to manufacture, and CDs cost about $6.00 (while this was going to drop greatly, the retail costs were not). The cost of LP and CD units that the record companies charged to retailers was approximately $10 for CDs and $6 for LPs, which resulted most retailers having a $6.00 mark-up for CDs and a $4.00 mark-up for LPs by most retailers. Typically, the consumer and the artists were being manipulated. The sound fidelity of CDs was horrible at first, but the consequential fascination and excitement was attributable to the medium and not the sound; therefore, the retail price of CDs was sustainable for the time being.

Why Pop Music Sucks

Around 1988, the personal computer made a grand, life-changing splash. At that time, personal computers were used largely for word processing, spreadsheets, and basic drawing, with memory in KBs. Computers came with a floppy drive, and soon thereafter, a disc drive. We connected to the world by way of our telephone landlines, which most of us do not even have anymore. In two years, the World Wide Web was going to change everything about our lives, and not just pop music. Our omnipresent analog world was no more.

What was it like to live in the 1980s?

- Tax rate for the wealthy top 1%: 47%
- Cost of a house in the San Francisco Bay Area:
  - $60K – $150K
- College tuition:
  - San Jose State University (SJSU): $500 annually
  - UC Berkeley: $1326 annually
  - Community Colleges: $5 per unit
  - Stanford: $6285 annually
  - University of Southern California (USC): $5420 – $13,446 (USC tuition increased from the first figure and throughout the decade to end up with the second figure)

Chapter Two
The 1950s
The Birth of Rock and Roll

In the 1950s American South, the segregation of white and black folks was the norm, and lynching was still common. However, just because black and white kids did not go to the same schools or drink from the same water fountains did not mean that they did not play together. According to Jennifer Ritterhouse in her book *Growing Up Jim Crow,* "Black and white kids interacted often, some every day, their encounters unfolding in yards, on streets, and in other spaces between the highly segregated zones of school and church and parlor." Ritterhouse continues, "Black and white children growing up in the Jim Crow South learned a great deal about race through their ongoing interactions with one another." White and black kids actually lived in the same neighborhoods and would "cross the tracks" to hang out together. According to an African-American interviewee for Ritterhouse, "...sometimes if they got hot [white children at play getting angry about something while playing with black children] they would run home and call us an [n-word], and my younger brothers would call them rednecks or peckerwoods and that was the end of that. The next day, they was back playing again, So we never got into any big problem about that." Developing from this arrangement during everyday existence, it would only be only a short time until racially distinct demographics came together and created a wholly new form of musical expression: Rock and Roll.

Musically, before Rock N Roll, there was country, rhythm & blues, jazz, classical and pop (see terms in glossary). By pop, I largely mean entertainers like Frank Sinatra and Lawrence Welk. In the South, country music was and still is "king." Black folks and their families were and are surrounded by this music every single day of their lives, and it would be only a matter of time for someone to grow up in the black community with a great appreciation for country music—someone who learned how to play guitar and had a natural high IQ for youthful subject matter to use as a source for lyrics. That part-time construction worker was a man named Chuck Berry.

Black rhythm & blues artists, of course, contributed to Berry's development, but up to then in the 50s, there was a very clear delineation in the way a black artist sounded and how a white artist sounded. Elmore James, T Bone Walker, Lighting Hopkins, Howlin' Wolf, Muddy Waters, and John Lee Hooker all sounded black, and it was easy to tell that they were. Black artists of the early 1950s were primarily blues and/or jazz artists, and white artists of the 1950s were largely country and folk artists. Black pop artists and jazz singers like Nat King Cole and Roy Hamilton were around as well. However, what happens when a young black man comes up with a combination of country tunes laced with R&B guitar riffs and solos, and he sings like a country singer?

Essentially, Chuck Berry created Rock N Roll with these criteria:

- Country song structure
- Black R&B guitar riffs and lead playing
- Youth-oriented lyrical subject matter
- Sing like Hank Williams or a country singer of the time (most, if not all, country singers were white at the time)

By 1957, another young man was going to force his way into superstardom. That individual was none other than Elvis Presley. Elvis' first manager, Sam Phillips was also going to be very important to the development of rock n roll. Sam and his Sun Records would record the pioneers of the genre: Howlin' Wolf, Jerry Lee Lewis, Johnny Cash, Carl Perkins, and Elvis Presley—and this was before anyone else. Elvis's parents had to sign with Sam Phillips for Elvis because he was not yet 18.

While Chuck Berry was a black guy who sounded "white," Elvis Presley was a white guy who sounded "black." Elvis was a young white artist who embraced the black rhythm and blues genre and black gospel music. He was influenced by black artists such as Roy Hamilton, and he essentially took whatever Chuck Berry did and simply put his unique character and signature on it. By the way, this was how things would work with all those to follow who put their unique character and signature into the development of the genre. The world was not going to be the same ever again because of the momentum of these changes. Rock and Roll was here to stay in whatever forms of it were to come in the future.

Now, a look into what made Rock N Roll: The Blues.

The blues form is the common thread in all 20th Century American music. Why was the blues unique to America? Amiri Baraka (previously known as LeRoi Jones) states in his book *Blues People*, "I have come to think about it, blues could not exist if the African captives had not become American captives." African American slaves were mostly prohibited from their free expression of things such as "political thought, native-tribal references, clothing, language, and drums." The access to, and use of native instruments was extremely limited. The slave masters believed that rhythmic drum patterns could be used subversively by slaves, so they prohibited the use of African drums. However, just because one's self-expression is suppressed does not mean that what they have inside of them cannot be expressed at all.

Therefore, when these slaves attempted to assimilate by adopting Anglo-European media of expression, such as the guitar, trumpet, piano, etc., the result was a cultural adaptation of instruments meant for European music theory combined with people who were not European. These people, these slaves, these beings who had been treated so inhumanly and who were regarded so consistently as inhuman, even by America's founding fathers, still retained pieces—however fragmented—of their true African native selves. Therefore, the former slaves managed to incorporate European music media even as they used music at the same time as a way to keep their African heritage alive.

Those native tendencies (cultural, artistic, social, etc.) upon confronting a completely hostile American culture created an explosion that did not develop instantly, but rather slowly over time like an ongoing experiment. Back in the day, if an African-American was singing an American folk song, that person may have felt that the melody line could have used a *minor 3rd* rather than a *major 3rd*. They did not necessarily know why, they just felt instinctively that their self-expression of themselves was more complete if they used that *minor 3rd*.

A major 3rd and a minor 3rd refer to the distances between two notes, which are measured in half-steps, the smallest tonal intervals between two notes in most musical cultures. A major 3rd is the distance of 4 half-steps, and a minor 3rd is the distance of 3 half-steps. Typically, the resulting relative sound between the two intervals causes the minor 3rd to be considered a bit "darker and/or a bit sadder" than the major 3rd. Another example would be if someone, such as the African-American mentioned previously, was playing a guitar. That person's innate cultural tendencies would direct him or her to shift the pitch of melodic notes up by a mere quarter-tone, which is half of a half-step. A guitar with its fixed fret positions would normally not be able to produce this type of melodic shift. However, if that person took a particular note on a string and "bent it" by tightening it within that same fret position, that quarter-tone or half-step upward shift could be produced.

This is the deal: someone from Europe did not plop down a stave sheet with the "blues scale" written on it in front of a 19th-century African American playing the piano, telling him or her to play that scale with feeling. The blues and jazz did not develop like that. Rather, blues and jazz were created by taking European musical concepts and reinterpreting them through one's experience as a slave, or as a descendant of slaves. The experiment created all sorts of rhythmic and harmonic extrapolations until we had a wholly new and unique form of music—the blues. Thomas Brothers quotes, "...the tip of a bottle, [break it off and sand it down] slip it over a finger, and drag it across the strings to make them whine and moan."

For us modern-day people, we can pull from our everyday experiences, particularly our bad ones, and play music with that emotion and feeling in our hearts. According to the great pioneering soprano saxophonist Sidney Bechet,

Brothers quotes further, "See how many ways you can play that note—growl it, smear it, flat it, sharp it, do anything you want to it. That's how you express your feelings in music."

As an important aside, former South American and Caribbean slave regions did not produce the blues, and this is because slave owners in those regions allowed their slaves to retain certain aspects of their African heritage, such as their music and percussion instruments. That is why the music from those former slave regions sound peculiarly African-influenced.

What was it like to live in the 1950s?

- People had these media forms:

    - Radio in the home and in cars
    - Record player
    - Telephones
    - Movie theaters
    - Live sports
    - Black and white TV
    - Portable transistor radios

- Tax rate for the wealthiest 1%: 91%
- Houses: median home price in California: $9,500
- Helmets, seatbelts, passenger laws non-existent

- College tuition:

  - SJSU: FREE
  - UC Berkeley: FREE
    (no, you are not hallucinating)
  - Stanford: $660 annually
  - USC: $640 – $960

Chapter Three
The 1960s
Pop Music College

The decade of the 1960s began innocently enough with "doo wop" vocal groups and other pop singers riding the Rock N Roll wave. Most of these artists were squeaky clean, and appealed to the common denominator: white folks. Elvis enlisted in the U.S. army. However, there was tragedy accompanying the new RNR soundtrack already, as such royalty as Buddy Holly, Richie Valens, and J.P. Richardson, AKA The Big Bopper, were killed together in a plane crash on February 3, 1959. Don McLean (1971) responded to this tragic event in the song "American Pie" where he repeats the phrase, "The day the music died." Fortunately, it was not actually the day the music died. However, I can understand why McLean may have thought of it that way at the time. When you lose three larger-than-life musicians in a nascent genre, it did indeed seem like the music had died, but it was going to live on.

Soon after, however, Patsy Cline and three others lost their lives in a very similar way. Patsy was 30 years old at the time of her death and was a brilliant singer who operated between the genres of country and RNR. Moreover, to join these tragic events, President John Fitzgerald Kennedy was assassinated. The Sixties were proved very tumultuous. However, good things were coming from across the Atlantic pond.

The Beatles consisted of John Lennon, Paul McCartney, George Harrison, and Ringo Starr. These four lads from Liverpool, England, together with their manager, Brian Epstein, and their producer, George Martin, were going to set the world ablaze with a new approach and a path forward for pop music. Whatever came about because of The Beatles did not exist at all before The Beatles, as they influenced the entire world of pop music from then on and changed the future of the genre forever.

How about the many other artists/musicians working at the time? There were many, and some of them were brilliant. Those brilliant individuals include:

- Bob Dylan
- Brian Wilson
- Berry Gordy
- James Brown
- Miles Davis
- John Coltrane

- Burt Bacharach
- Sly Stone
- Jimi Hendrix

Stephen Stills from Crosby, Stills, Nash & Young is quoted, "I followed [Jimi Hendrix] around for two years learning how to play lead guitar. I literally followed him like he was my guru. People thought I was a groupie, but that wasn't it. I was going to music school." [Facebook post May 28, 2023]

George Clinton from Parliament-Funkadelic fame is quoted, "I heard "Stand!" and it was like: man, forget it! And Sly was like all the Beatles and all of Motown in one." [Kaliss]

Eddie Van Halen is quoted, "If it wasn't for The Beatles my brother Al and I most likely would have ended up classical or jazz musicians." [Spike TV Guitar God Awards (2009)]

What was it like to live in the 1960s?

- Tax rate for the wealthy 1%: 91% - 74%
  (This reduction was attributable to President John F. Kennedy.)
- Average housing ownership: $11K – $30K
- Freeway speed limit: 70 miles per hour
- Helmets, seatbelts, passenger laws non-existent
- Drugs illegal yet very available. The *"27 Club"* is born, but blues great Robert Johnson will always be the honorary "First One" of the club.

- Abortion federally illegal
- College tuition:
  - SJSU: FREE
  - UC Berkeley: FREE

  (no, you are still not hallucinating)
  - Stanford: $1005 annually
  - USC: $960 – $1847

- Housing: nearly anyone could afford a place to live. If you could hold a job, you could easily afford to live somewhere on your own with no house mates. It was that simple.

- Technology-wise:

  - TVs were mainly black and white with only 7-12 channels
  - Rotary telephones only
  - From the mid-sixties, cassette tapes became a staple in most American homes.
  - Record players, of course
  - Radio, mainly AM; transistor radios
  - Reel-to-reel tapes and 8-track tapes were common, too. The 8-track tape configuration was largely for automobiles. There is a photo of Muhammad Ali playing 45s in his car; of course, he was not driving at the time.

- Most kids played a musical instrument. They began in elementary grades in public schools and onward through to adulthood. There were no rental fees as long as they borrowed the instrument from the school. Further, they had much more time to practice than kids today do.
- The pressure of particular socioeconomic factors such as those in the 2020s simply did not exist in the 1960's. Therefore, those kids—our future pop stars of the 1970s—had the space to become who they were going to become. They did not have to be concerned about getting into a "good college" and achieving a STEM [science, technology, engineering and mathematics] degree just so that they would be able to live somewhere relatively expensive within the U.S, and particularly in California. It was a kind of mass breeding ground of talent that was unhindered and unimpeded by future constraints. Further, specifically because they were unhindered, they were able to study The Beatles and all other contemporary artists carefully in such a way that they would end up producing the most eclectic and progressive catalog of pop music ever produced.

Chapter Four

The 1970s
"I Have Always Imagined That Paradise Will Be a Kind of 1970s"

Jorge Luis Borges has been quoted as saying "I have always imagined that paradise will be a kind of library." I love that quote, and I decided to modify it to convey my perceptions of the 1970s.

Anyone who was going to be signed to a major record label in the 1970s was a child of the 1950s and a student of the 1960s. All artists signed in the 70s came from an intense, concentrated musically scholastic environment, and within a period of around 15 years. In other words, from the 60s, which featured a relatively small number of major artists and influencers, came the 70s, which produced an incredibly eclectic and progressive catalog the likes of which has not been seen since. As opposed to what is seen at the time this book was written, nearly 70 years of modern pop music has resulted in most major pop artists sounding very similar to one another.

The main reason for this is the ways that consumers "buy" and listen to music because now they stream music in order to listen to it. Another reason is the recording technology, which currently involves push-button, digital technology that allows anyone to produce music tracks of their own with sampled sounds common to this period. These phenomena will be detailed further in later chapters, but if you want to check it out now, go for it: Chapter Seven: 2010s and Chapter Eight: 2020s. But for now, back to paradise.

In the 1970s, it was very common for major record companies to spend around $200,000 on an artist's recording. For the Carpenters' first album in 1969, *Offering* (aka Ticket to Ride), A&M recording company spent $100,000. The record did not really go anywhere, and there was talk of the Carpenters getting dropped. However, Herb Alpert, Co-CEO of A&M, decided to try releasing a single. That single was "Close to You," and it went all the way to number one. Safe to say that the Carpenters were not dropped after that, and A&M spent more than $100K on their next album.

A 1970s example is Gene Clark, a founder and an important member of The Byrds, and his 1974 album *No Other* cost $100,000. Unfortunately, Clark's album was not a commercial success, but, it has developed a special artistic appreciation due to the then-modern production techniques.

Pink Floyd's *Dark Side of the Moon* cost around $225,000, which sounds about right knowing that album and the band very well, but at the time, Pink Floyd was not the iconic band that we now know and revere. Their previous album was *Obscured by Clouds*; ever heard of it? I didn't think so. Therefore, it has been shown that record companies were willing to take risks with bands/artists in the supportive hope that something special would happen with their work eventually… and oftentimes it did indeed happen.

$100,000 USD does not seem like much by today's ultra-capitalistic standards, but consider this: in the 1960s, single-family homes in San Jose, California averaged approximately $15K-$30K. That's right—around $20K. Young homeowners would never dream of spending $100K on a home in the 60s. The value of the dollar meant different things back then. However, in the 1970s, single family homes were going to increase in cost to about $25K-$60K.

In 1970s California, kids in general, did not think a whole lot about going to a good college and then later going on to build a financial empire. For me, a certified misfit, my crowd and I never spoke about attending college or making sure that we all were going to be able to survive paying rent or mortgages or our future child's college tuition. Not once did I ever discuss this with my friends. Fast forward to 2024 when kids in San Jose and Cupertino, CA, are concerned constantly about their GPA, AP classes and tests, college transcripts and applications, getting into UCLA or UC Berkeley, etc. This type of constant focus and strategizing was unheard of in the 50s, 60s, and 70s, and these points are important to remember in terms of the development of what was coming within the music industry in the 1980s. Record companies, developing musicians, and artists had the time, space, and budget to perpetuate and advance the Golden Age of Pop Music.

So, paradise was on full display: all was analog with nothing digital, and everything was still affordable, including college, concerts, housing, weddings, transportation, gas, cars, movies, sporting events, and, of course, music lessons and instruments. All of these items were affordable in the 70s.

What was it like to live in the 1970s?

- Tax rate for the wealthy 1%: 50%
- Houses: average: $20K–$60K
- Les Paul Standard or Custom guitar: $350-$450
- Roe vs Wade passed in 1972
- Vietnam War ended in 1974
- Marvin Gaye releases *What's Goin' On* in 1970
- Color TV everywhere
- FM radio now a big thing
- Cassette recorders for copying, sharing, and studying
- College tuition: Because of California Governor Ronald Reagan's insistence on a major reduction in funding the state college system, free tuition was no more from 1975 and onward.

    - SJSU: $250 from 1975

- UC Berkeley: $600 from 1975
  - Community College: Still free
  - Stanford: $2400 annually
  - USC: $2004 – $4728

- Pop music TV shows:

  - American Bandstand
  - Ed Sullivan
  - Soul Train
  - In Concert
  - Don Kirshner's Rock Concert
  - The Midnight Special

Chapter Five
The 1990s
The 1996 Telecommunications Act Killed the Radio Star

At the beginning of MTV's reign, a song and video were released by The Buggles entitled "Video Killed the Radio Star." It was the very first music video that was aired on MTV. It was prescient for the time; however, it was not video that was going to kill the radio star, but rather President Bill Clinton and a Republican Congress. They were going to hammer a very pivotal nail into the coffin of traditional pop music, in which it would be laid to rest eventually. The 1996 Telecommunications Act was drawn up with visions of greater competition and less regulation. However, this Act negated much of what had constituted the 1934 Communications Act, and the Federal Communications Commission (FCC) which began in 1938, was focused on "diversity of ownership." Eventually, the FCC prohibited the ownership of multiple media stations for radio (AM or FM) and television (VHF or UHF), as well as any cross-ownership between radio and television. At first, the FCC wanted to bar ownership of two or more AM radio stations in a single market. Eventually, however, they barred any corporate ownership of more than one media entity in a single market, and this regulation was in place until the 1996 Telecommunications Act. After this major legislative change passed, all regulations barring the ownership of multiple media entities, outlets, stations, etc., were eliminated. Greater competition may have been a "selling point," but it was not at all the reality that this Act had created. The legislation allowed any corporation to invade any region in the country and buyout up to eight media networks across any media format.

Before the 1996 Telecommunications Act, a larger number of independent and corporate entities owned most media networks, hence, there was "ownership diversity." Before this jarring change in 1996, radio stations especially, were largely owned independently, and they were a major way for consumers to learn about the latest releases and pop music in general. The disc jockeys (DJs) would sift through the latest promotional pressings of a signed artist's latest releases in the form of physical 45's, LPs, CDs, etc. For record collectors, vinyl promo pressings are now very highly sought after because those pressings were the first to come off the pressing machines. First pressings are "valuable" because the original template called a stamper, was yet to be used and would ultimately degrade through continuous pressings.

The DJs were the experts. They were given far more autonomy before than after the Telecommunications Act. After the legislation, DJs became a "footnote" and sometimes did not even need to show up. Program directors became everything to the radio station, and therefore, they gutted any "soul" or competition to speak of in the radio industry. Conventional capitalistic efficiency is defined typically as "make as much money with the least amount of effort or resistance over time" (am I wrong?).

The bottom line for this 1996 Telecom Act was that corporations became the rulers of all media, and it was deemed that they should be allowed to buy out nearly as many media stations, networks, and other entities as they could afford, thereby eliminating any competition. That is why radio sucks now. No more AOR (album-oriented rock) and DJs being able to play and broadcast songs or recordings not released as singles. No more nights during which DJs featured rare recordings and bootlegs. No more DJs informing listeners about this or that new thing from so-and-so who had been influenced directly by this other so-and-so, and where the DJ would play songs from both artists one after another, or rather songs from both so-and-sos. From here on out, independent radio stations became very rare.

In other words, radio was an important media and cultural presence that educated the culture about music, especially when we were young. Radio was the go-to source for learning about current music and provided a space for listeners to think about and reflect upon music accompanied by knowledgeable guidance from the DJ—musical literacy. Now, all of that is gone.

Tommy James and the Shondells had a monster hit, "Crimson and Clover." It was mid-Summer 1968, and as a young up-and-coming artist, he was pleasantly shocked that a Chicago radio station "WLS" played a "rough mix" of "Crimson and Clover." Unsure of how the station gained access to the mix, but it launched a huge timeless psychedelic hit. That ain't going to be happening anymore.

What was it like to live in the 1990s?

- Tax rate for the wealthy 1%: 42% - 32% - 39%
- Houses: average $100K-$500K
- "Every family" has a computer
- File Sharing between "consumers" is now in full bloom
- Video games all day and all night
- Kurt Cobain changes everything in pop music
- Rap and Hip-Hop on a huge rise
- Politically, Rush Limbaugh and Fox News make their ascent
- College tuition:
    - SJSU: $1892 annually
    - UC Berkeley: $4139 annually

- Community College: $13 per unit
- Stanford: $14,280 – $23,058 annually
  Stanford tuition increased from the first figure and throughout the decade to end up with the second figure. USC's tuition increases 3.5% per year
- USC: $14,378 – $22,636

Chapter Six
The 2000s
The Serpent and
Its Fruit of Choice

Jon Bon Jovi is quoted as saying, "[Steve Jobs] is personally responsible for killing the music business." Even with countless meetings spent haggling with music industry heads and artists, Jobs still "charmed" his way into formatting iTunes (the answer to file sharing) by allowing the consumer to buy an artist's LP/album in piecemeal. It did not matter whether the song was a single or a track of incidental music/sound/noise. Consumers were now allowed to buy only singular tracks rather than the entire album. The industry had never before had a consumer option like this. Artists and recording companies found that they were suddenly making even less money than before. Yeah, it's legit—but you ain't making sh*t.

Let us go over why they were (are) making less money. When an entire LP was purchased, the artist and/or record company made publishing, mechanical, and writer royalties for every track on the album. The same was true for CDs, EPs, cassettes, 8-tracks, 45s, and singles with A & B sides. Therefore, when consumers were buying an LP, single, EP, CD, cassette, etc. and essentially possessing a copy of the work, the artist and publishing companies were being paid for all tracks, songs, periods of noise, or whatever else was part of the album in any of these media formats. That is why when iTunes allowed consumers to choose only those songs/tracks that they felt worthy of purchasing, it created an industry void of traditional, conventional, and proper monetization for music industry artists. The creation of iTunes was huge, and so was the 1996 Telecommunications Act. **Never forget** the way that these two events affected the music industry forever.

Jon Bon Jovi, I believe, was referring to the iPod, but I would say the iPod was not the main culprit here. Back then, we could separate tracks and create your own playlists because we were able to do that on our computers. Job's iTunes and other companies screwed everything up and continue to do so to this day by allowing consumers to "cherry-pick" or "apple-pick" what songs they want from an entire album without buying the entire album. I understand that buying a single—which should include the single itself and a B-side—was and is typical; however, if the consumer wants any of the other songs on the album, the consumer should have to buy the entire album.

Let's take a look at the socioeconomic factors of the time. It was noted in a previous chapter that homes in San Jose, CA during the 1970's were averaging 20K-60K. In the 2000's, multiply those 70s averages by a factor of 20: $400,000-$1,200,000. Moreover, twenty years later in the 2020's, home ownership costs twice as much as those averages in the 2000's. As for college tuition, it was always relatively more expensive to go to NYU, Columbia, Yale, Harvard, Stanford, USC, Princeton, etc., but all other "less expensive" colleges are far more expensive now, too, which means that those coveted colleges are astronomically more expensive.

So, what about wages? Have wages kept up? No... wages have not kept up. According to Robert Reich, economics professor emeritus at UC Berkeley:

> Before the 1980s, the main driver of profits and the stock market was economic growth. It was a virtuous cycle: Demand for goods and services generated more jobs and higher wages, which in turn stoked demand for more goods and services. But since the late 1980s, the major means by which corporations have increased profits and stock prices has been by keeping payrolls down. Studies show that prior to 1989, economic growth accounted for most of the stock market's gains. Since then, most of the gains have come from money that would otherwise have gone into the pockets of workers. All that has made the rich even richer. The richest 1 percent of the American households now own 50 percent of the value of stocks held by American households. The richest 10 percent

own 92 percent. But it has had the opposite effect for everyone else... less and less is going to worker wages and salaries.

What was once a virtuous cycle is now a vicious cycle. The great majority of real life-sustaining wages, income and wealth go to the top 1% of wage-earning individual, and that is without any "trickle-down" benefit. The additional and profound amount of salt in the wound—and what makes this issue less penetrable—is that those top 1% earners are involved equally in contributing to any politician who claims to maintain the status quo. In fact, they intend to keep it the same or make it even worse.

"American Idol." When this show began to air in 2002, cell phones were a complement to the programming because viewers could call in and give support for their favorite singer in the competition. "American Idol" became a weekly event in which it was common to have "American Idol" house parties hosted by neighborhood folks in every region of the U.S. Suddenly, singers became the unavoidable focus for those viewers who had never paid attention to singers in the past, and these people were now paying feverishly close attention to unknown singers like never before. This had both a direct and indirect effect on the remainder of the music industry. Guitar playing was going to fade into oblivion. Inadvertently, bands themselves would become an afterthought. Coincidence perhaps? I do not think so.

Another musical element was about to fade into oblivion as well: Orchestras are now heard rarely currently in pop music. From the beginning, when music and recording industries were in full swing with mass consumer activity, it was very common for artists' recordings to feature all configurations of orchestra and horn ensembles. Often, an entire album would feature a full orchestra in all its glory performing arrangements of various moods and colors. This type of recording was very common and kept many musicians employed. For example, strings and horns were intrinsic to most recordings. If a rock tune needed a bit of added emotional emphasis, a small orchestral arrangement would be added. For example, Grand Funk Railroad's song "Loneliness" had a hard rock/funk band featuring an entire orchestra to enhance (musically) the overall emotional execution. Do you ever hear that anymore? Not for the time-being. Yes, it is expensive, but so are videos, and in fact, videos are more expensive than producing an album. (What is more important: the music or the video?)

What was it like to live in the 2000s?

- Tax rate for the wealthy 1%: 39.1%
- Housing cost on average: $400K – $1.2 Million
- September 9, 2001: The 9/11 attack on our shores for the first time in a long time changed many things.
- Cell phone: might as well call it an appendage.

- Apple releases the iPod and iTunes. The serpent offers its fruit of choice, and we fervently accept.
- "American Idol" premieres
- Cable TV: 200+ channels
- Rap and Hip-Hop are *king*
- Music recording software was developing rapidly.
- This technology would change the industry forever.
- Video gaming is huge. Young people play these games for hours on end every possible chance they get. They were being re-wired for the times to come. By the way, what is it like to drive on roads and highways currently?
- College tuition costs:

    - SJSU: $3163 annually
    - UC Berkeley: $6802 annually
    - Community College: $26 per unit
    - Stanford: $24,441 – $38,700 annually
    - USC: $24,123 – $39,183

Chapter Seven
The 2010s
Technological Mis-Advantages

What were people carrying with them back then? CELL PHONES, 24/7. Essentially, the cell phone is a portable computer that makes phone calls. As far as music recording industry standards, the software of choice in the industry was and is Pro Tools, the leading first choice for engineers in the world. Unsurprisingly, musicians/artists recorded performances benefit from the digital technology, which had advanced greatly by this time. Any artist/musician who was "subpar" could now be "par." Anyone that sounds horrible in real life could sound "acceptable" on a recording. Further, if the artist/musician is already great, it just takes a little "nip & tuck," but not an entire face-lift. Generally, modern music consumers are satisfied with this advancement, but let us analogize this phenomenon to the case of professional sports. Imagine that digital kinesiology is a thing, and that any athlete, sub-par or just plain average, could enhance his/her athletic performance to the extent to which they could compete with actual professional-level athletes. Would that be acceptable for a sports fan? Many sports fans are music fans too, by the way. At this point, most, if not all, sports fans would be apoplectic about cheering on a team of digitally enhanced athletes. Thus, if professional athletes' digital enhancement is unacceptable, then why is the digital enhancement of professional musicians acceptable? The first reaction of sports fans (of which I am of one) is that these athletes are in a competitive environment, but so is everyone in the music industry. Both industries and markets are extremely competitive, and the sheer number of potential artists, singers, and musicians far exceeds the number of athletes who are competing for a finite number of positions. Therefore, digital enhancement increases the degree of competition in the music industry because anyone can compete.

Timing can be everything. Just look at the case of Rob Pilatus and Fabrice Morvan, Rob & Fab, of Milli Vanilli fame and shame. They were a late 80's phenomenon, a male duo, good-looking, who danced and knew how to entertain an audience. Their singing abilities were "okay," but not up to "par" with their competitors. German producer Frank Farian was the project's mastermind. However, Farian did not think that their singing was good enough for the tracks. Everything else was fine, but the vocals needed help. Accordingly, Farian got the idea of having other singers come in and do the vocal tracks instead. Those singers were John Davis, Charles Shaw, and Brad Howell. Farian had them sing all of the vocal tracks for both Rob and Fab, and Shaw handled the rap sections. Back then, you could keep this kind of thing more on the down-low; therefore, the single and album were both released, and with MTV at its height, the videos accompanying the songs were a smash hit. Thus, Milli Vanilli ended up winning a 1989 Grammy for Best New Artist.

Not long after their Grammy success, however, there was a very revealing event that occurred on July 21st, 1989, at an MTV event in Bristol, Connecticut, where the disc player, the duo were using to lip-synch to, began to skip right at the point where the lyric—which was supposed to be "girl, you know it's true,"—kept repeating as "girl you know it's, girl you know it's, girl you know it's...." Surprisingly, they finished their set without any other incidents and without their fans noticing what actually happened. Nevertheless, with the evidence of that Bristol event and other suspicions that were voiced, the duo had to admit that they did not sing on their own recordings.

The "shocking truth" about Rob Pilatus and Fabrice Morvan was that they were not good singers. The Grammy Academy was shocked, stunned, and incensed, and Milli Vanilli became the poster children of what not to do in the industry. Ultimately, their Grammy award for 1989 Best New Artist was pulled from their hands, and they were disgraced and shunned.

That is the summary of their story. Now, let us imagine Rob and Fab in the present (2024): young, good-looking, dancers and entertainers who could sing adequately, but not well. Visually, they have all the gifts to make a killer video. Sounds to me like they would fit in perfectly in 2024. In the 80s, they lacked the technology to properly augment their own voices. However, now they would have every digital tool and plug-in at their disposal. We would be able to hear Europeans Rob and Fab with their accents and their personal vocal inflections but with corrected pitch, timing, vibrato, etc. With the aid of auto-tune and Melodyne, bringing in other singers would not be necessary. Also, their modern fans would be fine with this arrangement because this is the way things work currently anyway. The modern music industry and all modern pop music icons accept that most, if not all, singers have used digital technology to correct or enhance their recorded performances.

So how about giving Rob—who is still around—and Fab's family (because Fab passed away, unfortunately) their Grammys back? Is there really that much of an ethical or moral differential between the two phenomena? One includes hired, outside singers because that was the only way to improve recorded vocal performances at that time, and the other has digital editing technology that allows anything to be corrected. What is the difference in the end? Why not give Milli Vanilli their Grammys back? There are many current singers and/or artists who could not exist without extensive digital correction and enhancement, and that is the standard now;

otherwise, you would have to have another singer come in and perform the tracks.

What was it like to live in the 2010s?

- Tax rate for the wealthy 1%: 35%
- Average house costs in populous areas in California: $500K – $1.7 Million
- College tuition costs:

    - SJSU: $3479 – $5472 annually
    - UC Berkeley: $10,000 – $17,160 annually
    - Community College: $46 per unit
    - Stanford: ~$47,331* annually
    - USC: $41,442 – $55,106

- Streaming revenues surpass physical sales for the first time in history. Spotify had a 100% increase from 2013 which was 78.6 billion streams.

---

* ~ = approximately; plus-or-minus

Chapter Eight
The 2020s Going Forward?

The Golden Age of Pop Music: 1955 – 2010

The end of the 20th century marked the end of conventional monetization within the music industry and ended the system with which the entire industry had operated from the beginning. That is all gone. The 21st century marks the beginning of digital streaming and the mass, passive consumption of music. With streaming, consumers/listeners are not actively listening; it is a passive activity at best. And by "active listening," I mean listening to an album or single song and not doing anything else at the same time. Way back when, we would digest the liner notes for the album or song and take note of who wrote the song(s), who produced the recording(s), where and when it was recorded, and who the musicians were who had played on it, as well as what record company was presenting the work. Yes, it was like that. Paul McCartney is quoted as saying: "When you bought an album… you saved up to buy this album… it was a huge event… you would take it out of this brown bag and you'd study it… and you'd read every liner note, and every little photo… so we [The Beatles] wanted to do something that was really a value for your money."

From the 1950s onward, the fact that consumers would buy an artist's work, bring it home, and play it many times over, would weigh on the minds of all parties involved in producing that work. Therefore, it was expected to have layers of perceptive elements that would be able to withstand such repeated listening. Sonic, harmonic, structural, lyrical, and instrumental density and complexity were all necessary and typical. However, here in 2024, most consumers—particularly those who are young —stream their music by allowing an algorithm to choose what gets played next. There is no expert DJ helping them. While DJs in a previous era would sift through the new releases for all of us in order to present what they had decided was worthy of airplay. There is nothing like that now. By the way, there are currently over 40,000 new releases every week in these modern times (according to some sources 100,000 a day). Could any human being actually sift through these releases so that you would not have to do it yourself? Does anyone have the time, for that matter? As for "new releases," that refers to any new music released through modern media, such as YouTube, Facebook, Instagram, Twitter, Spotify, Apple Music, iTunes, Amazon Music, or whatever is next, etc. Further, as an important aside, does anyone have the time to learn how to play a musical instrument at a professional level anymore?

Publishing rights are very important, long-standing, and complicated. We are hearing a lot about publishing rights lately. Justin Bieber just sold his publishing rights for his compositions up to January 2023 for $200 million. Publishing involves the control and distribution of compositions, compensation to composers, songwriters, and lyricists, and permissions. Royalties are payments due to the author of the composition and the owner of the original mechanical, physical medium (LP, CD, DVD, purchased song files, etc.). Before 2000, the royalty issue was rather boring but still very important to the financial well-being for the entire music industry. Therefore, when Steve Jobs formatted iTunes so that consumers did not have to purchase an entire album, that format cut sharply and directly into what was a given source of income in earlier times.

Currently, most consumers stream their music by way of streaming services and do not purchase the physical forms of those works—double-whammy, actually a *triple*-whammy. In fact, the only time that a mechanical royalty is applied to a streamed recording is when a "… user chooses to play a specific song on a streaming service." However, when other songs are streamed along with that chosen tune, those recordings do not generate mechanical royalties. Quadruple-whammy? The only people making money are streaming companies and Top 10 artists, and that's it.

Why Pop Music Sucks

So far, these artists have sold many, if not all, of their publishing rights to various publishing companies because of the various issues noted above, their age, and the fact that they ain't makin' sh*t for anything anymore.

- Bob Dylan
- Neil Young
- Bruce Springsteen
- Neil Diamond
- Tom Petty's estate
- David Bowie
- ZZ Top
- Steven Tyler
- Huey Lewis
- Justin Timberlake
- David Coverdale
- Nikki Six
- Nancy Wilson
- Jeff Porcaro's estate
- Richie Sambora
- Neal Schon, Steve Perry, and Johnathan Cain [Journey]
- Def Leppard
- David Crosby
- Alice Cooper

- Bob Marley's estate
- Tommy Shaw
- Chrissie Hynde
- Steve Winwood
- Kurt Cobain via Courtney Love
- Smokey Robinson
- Ray Charles' estate
- Blondie
- B52's
- Kenny Loggins
- Hall & Oates
- Justin Bieber
- Michael Jackson's estate
- Phil Collins, Tony Banks, and Michael Rutherford
- Graham Nash
- Katy Perry

It is 2024 now, and my prediction for the next decade beginning in 2030 is that most pop music will be created and produced through AI. Of course, a human will still be needed to input the particular parameters, such as a 13:31 minute piece based upon Genesis' early work circa 1971-1973. The lyrical content will be about someone dying in their sleep and what that person experiences as they are dying. The lyrics would be featured on only 33.67% of the piece. This technology has begun to be implemented already, and by the end of the 2020s, most pop music will be created with this approach. Mark my words, and here is why:

- Streaming is meant to be passive. Consumers do not know or really care what is being presented to them unless they are listening actively (remember what active listening means).
- Streaming services are going to get the idea to produce their own singles. Why pay out royalties to others when they could produce "music" with AI and have the royalties paid to themselves?
- Socioeconomic factors, such as increased housing costs, increased education costs, virtual gaming, virtual social media, and stagnant wages will affect everything going forward. We will not have the TIME, SPACE, and BUDGET to develop high-quality, creative, progressive music. This, unfortunately, is what we have to look forward to.

Furthermore, I believe AI's significance is being diminished by equating it to other forms of technology, such as the automobile, refrigerator, or cell phone. You might compare AI with these previously mentioned "lesser discoveries," but be forewarned that AI is not an airplane or a convection oven. It is wholly different, in that it is on a level equal to the discovery and innovation of fire. Hopefully, the human species will be able to control AI in the same way. The ability to control fire is just as important as fire itself, and the ability to control AI will be as important as AI itself.

What is it like to live in the 2020s?

- Tax rate for wealthy 1%: 37% (so far)
- Single family homes in the South Bay Area of California (Silicon Valley): ~$1.5 – $2.7 million
- College tuition: [up to 2023]

    - SJSU: $7,852 (to date)
    - UC Berkeley: $14,226 (to date)
    - Stanford: $59,838 (to date)
    - USC: $59,031 – $65,449 (to date)

- Cable TV: ~$200 every month
- Streaming services: ~$5–$65 (each; for now)
- Cell phones: ~$1000 every two years
- Personal computers and accessories: ~$1000–$5000
- Video consoles (hand-held and consoles): ~$100 – $600

- Video games (each): ~$40-$100
- Federal minimum wage: $7.25 (no change since 2009)
- California minimum wage: $15.50
- Gibson Les Paul Standard: ~$2500.00
  [TIME? SPACE? BUDGET? – WHERE? Hhmm?]
- Roe vs Wade repealed by the Supreme Court 2022
- Politically, it's a mess...it is in the worst state that it has ever been in America.
- Consumers listen to music via streaming services, YouTube, and others. The LP and record players make a retro and sentimental comeback, which in my opinion is superficial at best. Children, kids, teens, and college students *do not* actively listen to music. Pop music is now the background music to their busy lives.

Remember when the cost of a suburban home in the San Francisco Bay Area was about $20K, and producing an album cost around $100K (1960s)? At that time, buying a home was around 20% of the price of releasing an album. As we go through the subsequent decades, the cost differential in California has shifted as follows and has been joined by the cost of producing a video for a song and/or a video accompanied by a song on the average.

Decade	House	Album Release	Video Release

(All values are approximate averages with wide disparity of costs. Early values not adjusted for current real dollar value)

Decade	House	Album Release	Video Release
1960s	~$20K	~$100K	N/A
1970s	~$50K	~$250K	N/A
1980s	~$100K	~$400K	~$100,000
1990s	~$200K	~$500K	~$700K
2000s	~$500K	~400K	~$1 Million
2010s	~$1 Million	~$250K	~$1.5 Mil
2020s	~$2 Million	~$100K	~$2 Million

~ = approximately; plus-or-minus

For the very first time in pop music history, the cost of a house in the San Francisco Bay Area is more than the cost for a major label to produce an album. In fact, the numbers have reversed. Where buying a house in the 60s/70s was around 20% of producing an album; now in 2020s, making an album is 20% of buying a house. Further, the cost of a house is approximately what it costs to produce a music video. What does this mean? Homes and videos are ridiculously expensive, and the majority of the artist and a record company's budgets have shifted from producing music to producing video. This has resulted in the further watering-down of music over the production of the video. The concentration of production has shifted from the music to videos. It is much less about the music now—it is about the visual engagement, enticement, and addiction. Note, if all of this did not result automatically in added profit, they would not be operating like this at all. Therefore, major record companies are unwilling to spend money on an artist's or band's music because it does not generate more profit for most involved. Consumers do not listen to music; *they watch it*. So, music artists have to be more Milli Vanilli and less The Beatles.

California is the regional focal point, but the state is still the global entertainment capital where up-and-coming musicians and artists, as well as current veteran musicians and artists, need the time and space to do what they do. They had the time and space in the 50s, 60s, 70s, and 80s; however, now there are socioeconomic factors that have made it very difficult for artists to pursue their careers. We might postulate, "Well, if you are a talented individual coming from Kalamazoo, Michigan, you could just stay there and get noticed and get signed there." However, this isn't true—actually, you need to be where the "gatekeepers" are so that they can notice you. You need to be where word about your work reaches those gatekeepers. Further, you need to be in a place where it's as easy as possible for those gatekeepers to check you out. Therefore, to exist for a decent amount of time in the entertainment capital of the world, you have to be able to pay what it costs to live there. Unfortunately, California is another world in terms of the cost of living. Los Angeles is a bit more forgiving than the San Francisco Bay Area, but Los Angeles is still more expensive than most other regions in the United States (except for Manhattan, New York; Boston, Massachusetts; and San Francisco, California).

Chapter Nine
Anecdotage

Music Students and Teaching Guitar in 2024

During my first 25 years of teaching, most of my students were comprised of middle school and high school aged students. Some of those students practiced at least two hours a day, and some of them are even doing the music business thing right now. However, in 2024, most of my students are adults who are making a living currently or are retired. For the first time, I have a roster of students who are mostly working adults: In a word—weird.

There was an incident a while ago that was going to portent of things to come – when a 5th grader was unable to take lessons because he was too busy with his debate team. Lately, I have had students pause or quit because of the amount of work they had to spend on their school applications. No, not college applications… private high school applications! I just had a student quit because she/he was having a difficult time with life in general, and there are many other students engaged in far too many activities that distract them from music. Once, the mother of a middle-school student was absolutely pissed because I was five minutes late for a lesson at 7:30pm. She scheduled her young prince so extensively and tightly that if the schedule was disrupted by a five-minute delay of some sort, she would go absolutely ballistic, and that was at 8:00 in the evening (remember, this is a middle school student). Never have I ever experienced that before.

The last student I will mention is a high school student who is very talented; however, she has no time and space to work on her vocal and musical skills, and her parents will not allow her to expand her studies dedicated to her special talents. This is torturous for me. Anyone like her in the days of yore would probably be out front performing or gigging already—that is how talented she is. However, in 2024, high school students must focus only on getting into the college of their choice and devote all of their waking hours to academic endeavors. The talent exists, but it is hidden or suppressed.

Some might think that prodigies seen on YouTube or whatever platform could be the answer. Yes, prodigies are amazing and very entertaining. They have always been a thing, and prodigies are very important and essential to classical and jazz music. However, for pop music, individuals who are _not_ prodigious are absolutely necessary. Here is a short list of non-prodigies:

Why Pop Music Sucks

B.B. King
Johnny Cash
Chuck Berry
Elvis Presley
John Lennon
Paul McCartney
George Harrison
Ringo Starr
Karen Carpenter
Kurt Cobain
Janis Joplin
Peter Gabriel
Jim Morrison
Jimmy Page
James Jamerson
Phil Collins
Steve Hackett
Chris Squire
Marvin Gaye
Diana Ross
Boz Scaggs
Sly Stone
Waylon Jennings
Thom Yorke
Taylor Swift
Bernard Butler
Liam & Noel Gallagher

Tom Petty
Bruce Springsteen
Brian May
Neil Peart
Dolly Parton
Johnny Rotten
Iggy Pop
Lou Reed
David Bowie
John Bonham
Angus Young
Gino Vannelli
Duck Dunn
Steve Cropper
Stevie Nicks
Madonna
Lady Gaga
Janet Jackson
Sara Bareilles
Michelle Branch
Avril Lavigne
Alanis Morissette
David Grohl
Krist Novoselic
Cindy Lauper
Chrissie Hynde
Sting

Jerry Baiden

Stewart Copeland	Emilio Castillo
Andy Summers	Justin Timberlake
Andy Partridge	Michael Buble
Boz Scaggs	Steve Perry
David Byrne	Greg Rollie
Jeff Beck	Jerry Garcia
Leonard Cohen	Kirk Hammett
Blossom Dearie	Cliff Burton
Mike Stern	James Newstead
Greg Allman	Brett Anderson
Ronnie Van Zandt	Bill Bruford
Joni Mitchell	Robert Trujillo
David Crosby	Ed Sheeran
Neil Young	Dave Mustaine
Stephen Stills	Carlos Santana
Bob Weir Phil Lesch	Alanis Morissette
John Phillips	Eddie Van Halen
James Taylor	Dimebag Darrell
Ella Fitzgerald	Zack Wilde
Larry Carlton	Debra Harry
Robben Ford	Duane Allman
Allan Holdsworth	Steve Miller
Robin Trower	Tina Turner
Justin and Dan Hawkins	Billie Joe Armstrong
James Hetfield	Jerry Gaskill
Lars Ulrich	Ty Tabor
Graham Nash	Doug Pinnick

Robbie Robertson	Kenny Loggins
Cat Stevens	Roger McGuinn
Arianne Grande	Eric Clapton

Based upon this short list, would any of you be okay with *never* having heard any music from these non-prodigies? Think about all of the good and bad times when you reached for comfort and support from any of these artists' music, and then think about what it would be like to not have them there. Would that be okay with you? How does that make you feel?

Musical Appropriation

Accusing Bruno Mars of cultural musical appropriation must be one of the most ridiculously illogical, ignorant and dim-witted accusations of all time.

Definitions:

- Appropriation involves taking something "without authority or right," as Merriam-Webster explains.
- "The adoption, usually without acknowledgment, of cultural identity markers from subcultures or minority communities into mainstream culture by people with a relatively privileged status." [dictionary.com]

I don't like the idea of a particular race having complete dominion over a particular music genre in its evolved state. And note that I do not mean the origins of that genre. Yes, the Blues was created because African American slaves and former slaves had to cope with the fact that only European musical instruments were available to them, which they manipulated to more accurately express themselves. Also, there was no such thing as a blues scale.

How did Rock N Roll begin? The father of the genre was a black guy who sounded like a white guy, and its first superstar was a white guy who sounded like a black guy. And, here we are in 2021 complaining about a non-black guy sounding like a black guy. Really? Duck Dunn, who was one of the greatest RnB bass players of all time, was white; therefore, is that appropriation? Would Buddy Holly be accused today of cultural appropriation? The irony is that Holly was, at least to some promoters, "black." Yes: Upon hearing a Buddy Holly song, some people believed that he was black. Remember that people at that time did not have the overwhelming levels of visual engagement that we have today. By the way, Holly was great friends with Little Richard.

Is it considered appropriation if I, a third-generation Japanese-American born and raised in San Jose, California, happened to become a guitar player who plays nothing but classic rock and classic funk? If it is not, then why is Bruno Mars, who also grew up in America and soaked up all of its culture regardless of racial foci, considered guilty of appropriation? It's ridiculous. I would bet anything that Mars could just turn around and play MC5's "Kick Out the Jams" and kill it. Is that still appropriation? Have we come to a point where because I am Asian, I should play only "Asian music?" And for that matter, Japanese music only?

My point is that race or nationality should not even be a consideration if you are truly listening to music for music's sake. Unfortunately, the most important element in today's media environment is visuals. Today's music is usually accompanied by a video. It appears that if the image is not "appropriate" to the accompanying music, it is labeled automatically culturally and racially appropriated. We would not be discussing this issue in the 50s, 60s, or the 70s, because people *listened* to music; they didn't *watch* music. Music today is dysfunctional in the sense that artists are expressing themselves moreso visually than musically. It is soulless. Miles Davis was quoted as saying that Blossom Dearie was the most soulful white singer around. Was Blossom Dearie, who was as white as the driven snow, *appropriating* just because she was soulful? If you have soul, you have soul. What difference does it make where you are from or what the color of your skin is?

Solos and Improvisation

Instrumental music was featured typically in recordings from the very beginning of the music industry. In the 1920s, over a hundred years ago, jazz was the prevailing "pop music." As jazz was mostly an instrumental genre, where improvisation was a main feature, soloing and/or lead-playing was commonplace. Listeners were acquainted very well with this musical approach. Then, as the century progressed, all musical genres were being recorded: folk, blues, bluegrass, gospel, country, classical and chamber music, and tribal events. People would listen via radio, 78s, and live performances. At first, radio was a competitor to the recording industry. Of course, both were going to quickly learn to work together to create a very lucrative and symbiotic industry.

Soloing or improvisation is essentially a spontaneous melodic composition. Since all instrumental music had an instrumental treatment of melody, listeners (consumers) thought of improvisations as other ways to expand on the work's melody (because that is what it was and is). However, fast forward to the 1950s, where solos and lead-playing were featured at the beginning, middle, and end of most songs. Solos could be thought of as a break from the lyrical aspects of the song, where the subject paradigm is expanded upon by a melodic interpretation. The featured instrument was typically a piano, guitar, or a horn/wind instrument. Solo sections would take the listener somewhere else for a bit, and sometimes solos themselves became the main feature of a song, particularly for those players who were virtuosos in their abilities. Virtuosity is a level of playing that engages a listener emotionally (heart) and technically (intellect) at the same time.

All players can find themselves somewhere on the following spectrum.

Why Pop Music Sucks

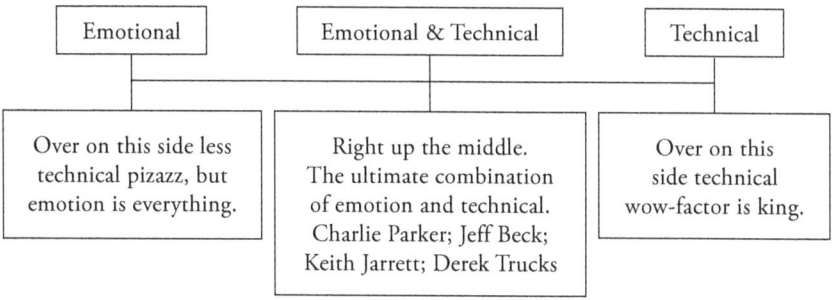

If you are a musician, where do you think you end up on this spectrum?

Video Games

I remember my nephews being given their very first Nintendo gaming consoles in 1983. At the time, I could not possibly have thought that this would be a major turning point for pop music. I was older and obviously had other things to deal with at that time in my life, so I did not adopt video games as part of my life and still do not. Gaming, however, was going to permeate nearly every part of my life and everyone else's lives as well going forward.

When I was a young teenager, anything I could define as a "passion" for me was basically the equivalent of what video games are for today's youth. For me, music was it. For others, it was automobiles, vocational occupations, small business, art, travel, culinary arts, drugs, crime, etc. Video gaming is like the most fun, rush-inducing, dopamine-laced activity under the sun. You do not have to be good or marginal to experience the immediate fun and enjoyment of playing video games. This immediacy is very important because it aligns directly against what it is like to learn how to play a musical instrument. The early stages of learning a musical instrument can be tortuous. I have reinforced constantly my student's mindset that learning an instrument takes everything that makes a very respectable individual: study, focus, diligence, efficiency, "do what you don't feel like doing (up to a point)," strategy, persistence, hard work, etc. Learning a musical instrument is very difficult and often a down-right wrenching thing to do. I am obviously not sugar-coating this for anyone. I am amazed consistently at the work ethic that is required to this day, and I have been playing for 47 years.

"Free time" for most young individuals, especially boys, in our modern times is split between video games and everything else. Beyond scholastic activities, the portion of "free-time" is key in understanding what has happened to pop music. When a young, talented kid/teenager is splitting their time between music and video games, they are watering-down their abilities for musical execution. Over time (it's been 40 years so far), this can only result in "negative results" in regard to music.

When I began writing this book, I did not think video games had that much of an effect on the music industry or rock n roll. Then, I did the research for the book. And now, I'm a believer (Monkees reference) that video games *are* one of the largest factors involved with the demise of rock n roll and the deterioration of pop music. Here is the deal: since many male children are more likely to be constantly engaged with video games, those particular boys, on average, are not going to become great guitar players or musicians. Period. The problem with video games, is time and space. These elements are required for the learning process. Without those elements, you are going to be sub-par. Seriously. If John Lennon and Paul McCartney were to have split their free time up with video gaming, they would not have had the time and space for writing songs and learning how to play various instruments. No way. Therefore, we would never have had The Beatles. Cool? I don't think so...

Recording Technology Through the Decades

Recording music and voice began with excitement and it has remained exciting since its origins. Every decade has produced changes, advancements and innovations that have colored the modern music listening landscape. Here is a summary of recording technologies since the 1950s:

- **1950s**: Studios employed 2-track recording on magnetic tape machines. The tape was a 1/2 inch 2-track. Musicians were in the same room typically, where they were isolated minimally from each other. Much of the time, there was only one mic recording the entire group—maybe, four mics at the most. The room where the musicians were placed was very important as well. How the musicians were positioned and how they were positioned in relation to each other was also pivotal to the process, as well as of course, the placement of the mic(s).

- **1960s**: Most of the time, recording involved 4-track, 1-inch tape machines. 8-tracks emerged later in 1968. For artists and producers, there had to be a strategy for using only four tracks. The Beatles is a definitive study of the way that this was accomplished. Imagine having to record four musicians together or separately, playing different instruments and/or singing. There must be room for background vocals and other feature instruments, and sometimes orchestration was needed… all on four tracks. Every square inch had to be assigned a recorded element strategically to fit everything onto the track, which meant that whatever was granted space on the tape was supposed to be there. Any audio element that was not up to the level that was needed would not make it onto that tape, or the album. The common technique was "bouncing," in which they would take an instrument recorded on one track and another instrument recorded on another track and combine them, essentially "mixing as you record" on another track. This would make room on the original tracks from which the two instruments came from.

- **1970s**: The 70s brought more tracks in the form of 16-track/1-inch and 24-track/2-inch machines.

24/2 was the standard. The techniques from the 60s were still being used together with the all-analog, valve-powered outboard gear from previous periods. With more tracks came more separation, and you didn't have to bounce as much. However, a technique that needs to be explained here is "splicing." This is the archaic form of editing, where you would join two separate recordings together. Before digital technology, this was done by hand. You would cut tape with a razor blade at a diagonal angle across the face of the tape, and then you would join the two segments together by cutting the other segment with a properly facing angle before "taping" them together.

- **1980s**: Analog was still the go-to recording environment, but digital technologies would make an important entry in the 1980s. Many times, two 24-track/2-inch machines would be synched together to offer 48 tracks at one time—and yes, you could still bounce and splice as before. Digitally, drum machines, keyboards, outboard gear, and other toys were going to create a very defining sound for the 80s. The Linn drum machine, which used sampled drum sounds and was linked digitally by way of a thing called MIDI, can be heard on many 80s' hits. In the 80s, digital meant toys. However, in the 90s, digital was also going to mean recording.

- **1990s**: Analog tape machines still dominated, but digital technology was gaining with DAT (Digital Audio Tape) recorders, SMPTE time code (Society of Motion Picture and Television Engineers), better sampling of sounds, and more digital instruments. Essentially, the 90s recording technology included a hybridization of analog and digital.
- **2000s**: Pro Tools was born, even though its first appearance was in 1990 as "Sound Tools." Where the 80s had digital toys, the 90s had digital recording, and then in the 2000s, computer software was going to make its presence known and be at the top of what most recording studios would be using from then on.
- **2010s**: Digital software plugins are now the bomb. This is the age of auto-tune and Melodyne together with with every possible type of keyboard plugin that gives the musician and producer any sound they could possibly think of. Want bass patches, want strings, want percussion patches, and want every possible B3, Rhoades, and piano sound, in any acoustical environment? No problem!
- **2020s**: Do-It-Yourself technology that allows anyone with any level of talent to record and present music is now the norm, as long as one knows how to operate in that digital eco-system. Digital technology is very affordable at this time (compared to everything else).

Chapter Ten
Special Additional Chapter

The Golden Age of Pop Music involves the birth of Rock N Roll (1950s); the childhood (1960s); adolescent period of existence (1970s); adult period (1980s); and the middle-age, "get off my lawn" period (1990s). The 2000s is the weakened and end-of-life, diaper-changing, hospice period of Rock N Roll. We could think of the 2000s as a transition period where Rock N Roll's end drew nigh. You may have your day in the sun, but you will inevitably set with the sun, as well.

This chapter is for all of you who have already read this book. I can only imagine what is going through your heads by now.

Here are the most important points that led to the pop music we have now:

1) Time, Space, and Budget: to become a highly skilled musician and/or singer-songwriter takes a ridiculous

amount of time, space, and budget. This point is first and foremost.

2) Video games: From 1983, our future musicians were going to split their "free-time" with video games, which means that the amount of time devoted to the endeavor of playing a musical instrument at a high level has been reduced, and the result is less traditional mastery. In other words, if Charlie Christian, T Bone Walker, Chuck Berry, Elvis Presley and Scotty Moore, B.B. King, Paul McCartney, John Lennon, Ringo Starr, George Harrison, Jimmy Page, Eric Clapton, Charlie Parker, Jimi Hendrix, Kurt Cobain, Eddie Van Halen, et al. had split their time equally among playing their instruments with playing video games, we would not have the memory and influence of these prized and honored musicians within our current lives. No way.

3) The 1996 Telecommunications Act: a huge, rusty, staph-ridden nail-in-the-coffin. This is unique to America. The United States is the only region in the world with this type of "regulation," which greatly favors, corporations, and ultimately reduced any musical literacy among ourselves and our youth. Americans no longer have DJ expertise as our guide. Therefore, our youth in middle-school, high school, and college have very little or no musical literacy. When I was in the 6th grade, I could rattle off the radio stations and their DJs that I regularly listened to, as well as

everything else I listened to. Ask a 2024 6th grader what and who they regularly listen to.

4) Apple iTunes: a monetary nail in the coffin. This ruined the conventional monetary model for the industry. No longer are "units sold" as a source of income, and by units, I mean LPs, cassettes, CDs, DVDs, 45s, and 8-tracks. Essentially, this has led to veteran, seasoned musicians/artists selling off their publishing rights to independent publishing companies, i.e., Bob Dylan, Neil Young, Bruce Springsteen, Alice Cooper, etc.

5) Streaming services: Essentially, criminal, unsympathetic companies fronting as music streaming services ["just kidding"]. They had strategically arranged things so that they would not have pay out royalties to artists that get algorithmically streamed along with other artists.

6) The Wanton Greed of Capitalism: Capitalism helped it along at first, and then, helped kill it.

After this section, there will be "blank pages." Write directly on these blank pages. I want you to fill them with your thoughts and feelings. What is happening with you and your relation to pop music and things around it? If this is a borrowed book, like from a library (aka Paradise), please make sure to leave room for others. Write and have fun...

- Which decade would you like to travel back to, and why? What would make you not want to come back to the present, and what would make you want to come back?
- Which non-prodigies could you not live without?
- What do you think the tuition for your college of choice or as an alum will be in ten years? Twenty years from now?
- What do you think the tax rate should be after anyone accumulates at least $5 million for the year? For the New Deal, this would have been 94% for whatever the wealthy made over $300,000 (in 1930s' USD). Now, it is around 36%.
- Do you like the idea of using AI to create pop music?
- Is any of this sustainable?

Special Additional Chapter

Special Additional Chapter

Special Additional Chapter

Special Additional Chapter

Glossary

27 Club: The 27 Club is an informal list that consists largely of popular musicians, artists, actors, and other celebrities who died at age 27.

8-Track Tape: 8 tracks are a continuous loop of tape. They did not need to be turned over to keep playing. There were four programs of music on each tape with two tracks on each program to create stereo sound.

American Bandstand: Abbreviated AB, is an American music-performance and dance television program that aired regularly in various versions from 1952 to 1989, and was hosted from 1956 until its final season by Dick Clark, who also served as the program's producer. It featured teenagers dancing to Top 40 music introduced by Clark.

Analog: Not digital: not computerized; usually involves tube/valve powered equipment.

Antenna: A usually metallic device (such as a rod or wire) for radiating or receiving radio waves.

Appropriating or Appropriation: To take or make use of without authority or right.

Auto-Tune: A software plugin that corrects flaws on vocal tracks.

Bass: Being of deep, low pitch and tone; a 4-string instrument (typical) acoustic or electric.

Beat Detective: A software plugin that corrects flaws on drum tracks.

Black Rhythm & Blues: A specific form of the blues that involves electric instruments and a drum kit and performed by black artists.

Blossom Dearie: Margrethe Blossom Dearie (April 28, 1924 – February 7, 2009) was an American jazz singer and pianist.

Blues: A uniquely American form of music created out of former slaves expressing themselves through European instruments.

Bruno Mars: Peter Gene Hernandez (born October 8, 1985), known professionally as Bruno Mars, is an American singer, songwriter, and record producer.

Buddy Holly: Charles Hardin Holley (September 7, 1936 – February 3, 1959), known as Buddy Holly, was an American singer and songwriter who was a central and pioneering figure of mid-1950s rock and roll.

Burt Bacharach: Burt (Freeman) Bacharach, 1928–2023 American songwriter.

California: A state of the southwestern U.S. on the Pacific, the nation's most populous state.

Capitalism: An economic system that favors private and corporate enterprises providing most societal necessities, and also results in a great disparity between the wealthy and non-wealthy.

Carpenters: Brother-sister duo of Richard and Karen Carpenter in the 1970s with hits such as "Close to You," "Superstar," and "Rainy Days and Mondays."

Cassette: A plastic cartridge containing magnetic tape in which the tape passes from one reel to another.

CD: A small optical disk usually containing recorded music or computer data.

Choreography: The composition and arrangement of any type of dance.

Consumer: A person who purchases and utilizes economic goods.

Country: Music derived from or imitating the folk style of the Southern U.S. or of the Western cowboy.

DAT: Digital audiotape.

Digital: something (such as a device) characterized or operated by digital technology.

Disc Drive: A device for reading and writing data on a magnetic disk.

Distract: To draw or direct (something, such as someone's attention) to a different object or in different directions at the same time.

DJ: Disc Jockey; An announcer of a radio show of popular recorded music.

Don Kirshner's Rock Concert: An American television music variety show that ran during the 1970s and early 1980s, created and produced by Don Kirshner and syndicated to television stations, initially through Viacom Enterprises, and later through Syndicast.

Drums: A percussion kit consisting of a bass drum, snare, hi-hat, cymbal, and tom drum; it can have many configurations of those elements.

Duck Dunn: Donald "Duck" Dunn was an American bass guitarist, session musician, record producer, and songwriter. Dunn was notable for his 1960s recordings with Booker T. & the M.G.'s and as a session bassist for Stax Records.

Dynamics: The relative volume fluctuations and changes within the span of a musical work.

"Ed Sullivan Show": an American television variety show that ran on CBS from June 20, 1948, to March 28, 1971, and was hosted by New York entertainment columnist Ed Sullivan.

Elvis Presley: Elvis Aaron Presley; 1935–1977 American singer; first rock and roll superstar.

Engineer: recording engineer.

File Sharing: Peer-to-peer file sharing is the distribution and sharing of digital media using peer-to-peer (P2P) networking technology. P2P file sharing allows users to access media files such as books, music, movies, and games using a P2P software program that searches for other connected computers on a P2P network to locate the content desired.

Floppy Disk: A thin plastic disk coated with magnetic material on which data for a computer can be stored.

Gatekeeper: a person or thing that controls access to something, i.e. literary agent.

Gene Clark: Harold Eugene Clark (November 17, 1944 – May 24, 1991) was an American singer-songwriter and founding member of the folk-rock band The Byrds.

Genesis: One of the greatest progressive rock bands of all time; from Surrey, England.

Guitar: A flat-bodied stringed instrument with a long-fretted neck and usually six strings played with a pick or with the fingers

Horn Section: A relatively small ensemble of horn instruments, such as a trumpet, tenor sax, trombone, etc.

"In Concert:" A late-night television series that Don Kirshner created. Hosted by Don Branker, the series was a showcase for bands of the era to be taped "in concert" and then broadcast on ABC on Friday nights.

iPod: iPod is a pocket-sized portable music-playing device produced by Apple; iPods can store several thousand songs, the exact number of which depends upon the model.

iTunes: iTunes is a software program that acts as a media player, media library, mobile device management utility, and the client app for the iTunes Store

Jim Crow: The Jim Crow laws were state and local laws introduced in the Southern United States in the late 19th and early 20th centuries that enforced racial segregation. "Jim Crow" is a pejorative term for an African-American. Such laws remained in force until the Civil Rights Act was passed in 1964.

John F. Kennedy, President: John Fitzgerald Kennedy (May 29, 1917 – November 22, 1963), often referred to by his initials JFK, was an American politician who served as the 35th president of the United States from 1961 until his assassination in 1963.

Jorge Luis Borges: 1899–1986 Argentinian author.

Karen Carpenter: Born in Connecticut on March 2, 1950. Lead singer for the Carpenters. Died February 4, 1983 from anorexia nervosa.

KB: Kilo-byte; a unit of computer information equal to 1024 bytes.

Keyboards: Any combination of piano-like instruments, such as organ, Fender Rhoades, Wurlitzer, synthesizers of all types, both analog and digital

Lynching: Widespread practice of extrajudicial killings which began in the United States' pre–Civil War South in the 1830s and ended during the civil rights movement in the 1950s and 1960s. Although lynching victims were members of various ethnicities, after roughly 4 million enslaved African Americans were emancipated, they became the primary targets of white Southerners.

MC5: An American rock band from Lincoln Park, Michigan, formed in 1963. The original band line-up consisted of vocalist Rob Tyner, guitarists Wayne Kramer and Fred "Sonic" Smith, bassist Michael Davis, and drummer Dennis Thompson.

Mechanical Royalties: Each time a musical composition is reproduced, whether physically or digitally via on-demand streaming or download-to-own services, composition owners (i.e., songwriters and their publishers) are paid. Mechanical royalties will often flow from the owners of master copyright's owners (i.e., record label) to songwriters.

Melodyne: Melodyne is pitch correction software that works by receiving recorded audio and analyzing the pitch and tempo. It then separates the notes into blobs, which you can then edit individually as necessary. [Sweetwater]

Metal: A genre of rock music that developed in the late 1960s and early 1970s, largely in the United Kingdom and United States. With roots in blues rock, psychedelic rock and acid rock, heavy metal bands developed a thick, monumental sound characterized by distorted guitars, extended guitar solos, emphatic beats and high volume.

MIDI: Abbreviation for Musical Instrument Digital Interface. It is a protocol that allows computers, musical instruments and other hardware to communicate.

Miles Davis: Miles Dewey Davis III **(May 26, 1926 – September 28, 1991)**. Trumpeter and extremely influential American jazz musician.

Motown: The Motown sound, is a style of rhythm and blues music named after the record company Motown in Detroit, where teams of songwriters and musicians produced material for girl groups, boy bands, and solo singers during the 1960s and early 1970s.

Muhammad Ali: 1942–2016; originally Cassius Marcellus Clay; greatest American boxer of all time; died from Parkinson's.

New Deal: the legislative and administrative program of President Franklin D. Roosevelt designed to promote economic recovery and social reform during 1933–1940. The wealthy were taxed 94% for every dollar after $300,000 (not adjusted).

Orchestra: A group of musicians that included in particular string players organized to perform ensemble music

Outboard Gear: Used to process or alter a sound signal separately from functionality provided within a mixing console or a digital audio workstation. Outboard effects units can be used either during a live performance or in the recording studio.

Paul McCartney: Founding member of The Beatles, together with John Lennon, George Harrison, and Ringo Starr created the greatest and most influential band of all time

Pirate Bay: The Pirate Bay is a file-sharing Web site founded in 2003 by the Swedish anti-copyright group Piratbyrån ("Bureau of Piracy"). It is the most popular site to use BitTorrent, a protocol that allows the distribution of large files.

Pitch: The property of a sound and especially a musical tone that is determined by the frequency of the waves producing it; highness or lowness of frequency.

Plug-in: Computer software that adds new functions to a host program without altering the host program itself; used widely in digital audio

Pop Music: A genre of popular music that originated in the West during the 1950s and 1960s. Pop music is eclectic, and often borrows elements from urban, dance, rock, Latin, country, and other styles. Typically, songs are short to medium-length with repeated choruses, melodic tunes, and hooks.

Pro Tools: Computer software for recording music; it is an eco-system including many plugins and other digital outboard gear.

Producer: A person who supervises and brings together all elements of music production, which can include basic song ideas and arrangements, scheduling, choice of musicians, recording, editing... everything.

Promoter: A person involved in the promotion of an artist, singer or band; or a company involved in promoting a particular venue or event.

Publisher: A publisher is the owner and administrator of the copyrighted work, who has control over the songs/works; However, publishing is 50% of total monetization; the other 50% is the writer's share.

Punk: A loud, fast-moving, and aggressive form of rock music, popular in the late 1970s and early 1980s. [Oxford]

Recording Company: Manages such brands and trademarks, coordinates the production, manufacture, distribution, marketing, promotion, and enforcement of copyright for sound recordings and music videos, while it also conducts talent scouting and development of new artists, and maintains contracts with recording artists and their managers.

Rock: A form of popular music that evolved from rock and roll and pop music during the mid and late 1960s. Harsher and often self-consciously more serious than its predecessors, it was characterized initially by musical experimentation and drug-related or anticstablishment lyrics.

Royalties: Music royalties are compensatory payments received by rights holders (songwriters, composers, recording artists, and their respective representatives) in exchange for the licensed use of their music.

Sam Phillips: Samuel Cornelius Phillips (January 5, 1923 – July 30, 2003), better known as Sam Phillips, was an American record producer who played an important role in the emergence of rock and roll as the major form of popular music in the 1950s (Sun Records).

Segregation: The separation or isolation of a race, class, or ethnic group by enforced or voluntary residence in a restricted area, by barriers to social intercourse, by separate educational facilities, or by other discriminatory means.

Single: A song that is released separately from an album, although it usually also appears on an album. In other cases, a recording released as a single may not appear on an album.

SMPTE: Uses computers to synchronize separate audio and video playback, or multiple audio tape machines perfectly. In this system, one track of each machine carried the timecode signal, while the remaining tracks were available for sound recording.

Sony: A Japanese multinational conglomerate corporation headquartered in Minato, Tokyo, Japan. As a major technology company, it operates as one of the world's largest manufacturers of consumer and professional electronic products, the largest video game console company and the largest video game publisher. Through Sony Entertainment, it is one of the largest music companies (largest music publisher and second largest record label) and the third largest film studio, making it one of the most comprehensive media companies. It is the largest technology and media conglomerate in Japan

"Soul Train:" An American musical variety television show. After airing locally on WCIU-TV in Chicago, Illinois for a year, it aired in syndication from October 2, 1971, to March 25, 2006. Over its 36-year history the show primarily featured performances by R&B, soul, and hip-hop artists. The series was created by Don Cornelius, who also served as its first and longest-serving host and executive producer.

Stamper: The template for a vinyl LP pressing, which is typically around 60,000 pressings.

Streaming: Relating to or consisting of the transfer of data (such as audio or video material) in a continuous stream particularly for immediate processing or playback.

Sun Records: An American independent record label founded by producer Sam Phillips in Memphis, Tennessee on February 1, 1952. Sun was the first label to record Elvis Presley, Charlie Rich, Roy Orbison, Jerry Lee Lewis, Carl Perkins, and Johnny

Cash. Phillips loved rhythm and blues and wanted to bring it to a white audience

Synching: By way of SMPTE, up to three 24 track tape machines could be made to work together to create a canvas of more tracks available to the production of a music recording

"The Midnight Special:" An American late-night musical variety series broadcast originally on NBC during the 1970s and early 1980s, created and produced by Burt Sugarman.

Track: A "lane" of magnetic particles on a reel of recording tape; the recording tape could have a number of lanes: 2 tracks, 4 tracks, 8 tracks, 16 tracks, and 24 tracks. For digital recording, the number of tracks is unlimited

Trickle-Down Economic Theory: The idea, suggestion at best, that "giving generously" to the wealthy will result in a downward flow of said wealth. It has never happened

Tuition: The price of or payment for instruction; particularly for college

Unit: A single thing or group that is a constituent of a whole, such as an LP, CD, EP, Cassette, DVD, etc.

Valve: A vacuum tube consisting of two or more electrodes in a vacuum within an airtight glass envelope or casing.

Virtual Reality: Virtual reality (VR) is a simulated experience that employs pose tracking and 3D near-eye displays to give the user the feeling of being immersed in a virtual world. VR applications include entertainment (particularly video games), education (such as medical or military training) and business (such as virtual meetings). Other distinct types of VR-style technology include augmented reality and mixed reality, referred sometimes to as extended reality or XR, although definitions are currently changing because of the nascence of the industry.

Walkman: Small portable cassette or CD audio player listened to by means of headphones or earphones

Bibliography

Are Violent Video Games Ruining Our Young Generation? https://www.ukessays.com/essays/young-people/are-violent-video-games-ruining-our-young-generation.php. Accessed 25 Mar. 2023.

Average Gas Prices in the U.S. Through History. 29 Dec. 2016, https://www.titlemax.com/discovery-center/planes-trains-and-automobiles/average-gas-prices-through-history/.

Baraka, Amiri. *Blues People: Negro Music in White America.* 1st Quill ed, William Morrow, 1999.

BBC Legends: Herb Alpert, Tijuana Brass And Other Delights (Edited) (2010). www.youtube.com, https://www.youtube.com/watch?v=us4TBtlbrcQ. Accessed 8 Apr. 2023.

"Blossom Dearie Was 'The Only White Woman Who Had Soul.'" *Vinyl Me, Please*, https://www.vinylmeplease.com/blogs/magazine/blossom-dearie-liners. Accessed 24 Apr. 2023.

Bosso, Joe. "How I Wrote 'Crimson and Clover.'" *Guitar Player*, vol. 57, no. 9, Sept. 2023, p. 98.

Brothers, Thomas. *Louis Armstrong's New Orleans*. W.W. Norton, 2006.

Chilton, Martin. "Recording Studios: A History Of The Most Legendary Studios In Music." *uDiscover Music*, 25 July 2022, https://www.udiscovermusic.com/in-depth-features/history-of-recording-studios/.

CJCJ. "Here Are the Faces and Real Singers of Milli Vanilli [PHOTOS]." *99.9 KTDY*, 9 Jan. 2021, https://999ktdy.com/here-are-the-faces-and-real-singers-of-milli-vanilli-photos/.

"Colleges in California." *CollegeDroid*, https://www.collegedroid.com/states/california. Accessed 25 Mar. 2023.

Contributor. "iTunes: A Look at Apple's Media App and Its Influence on an Industry." *Macworld*, https://www.macworld.com/article/227143/15-years-of-itunes-a-look-at-apples-media-app-and-its-influence-on-an-industry.html. Accessed 25 Mar. 2023.

Covert, Adrian. "A Decade of iTunes Singles Killed the Music Industry." *CNNMoney*, 25 Apr. 2013, https://money.cnn.com/2013/04/25/technology/itunes-music-decline/index.html.

Douris, Raina. "The First 100 Videos Played On MTV." *NPR*, 30 July 2021. *NPR*, https://www.npr.org/sections/world-cafe/2021/07/30/1021813462/the-first-100-videos-played-on-mtv.

Giacomozzi, Andréia Isabel, et al. "Experiences of Violence among Students of Public Schools." *Journal of Human Growth and Development*, vol. 30, no. 2, June 2020, pp. 179–87. *DOI.org (Crossref)*, https://doi.org/10.7322/jhgd.v30.10365.

Guralnick, Peter. *Last Train to Memphis: The Rise of Elvis Presley*. Little, Brown, 1994.

Herb Alpert - Signing the Carpenters to A&M. www.youtube.com, https://www.youtube.com/watch?v=T0rNeiy65tE. Accessed 8 Apr. 2023.

Hull, Jay G., et al. "A Longitudinal Study of Risk-Glorifying Video Games and Reckless Driving." *Psychology of Popular Media Culture*, vol. 1, no. 4, Oct. 2012, pp. 244–53. *DOI.org (Crossref)*, https://doi.org/10.1037/a0029510.

"John Davis: True Milli Vanilli Singer Dies from Covid Aged 66." *BBC News*, 26 May 2021. *www.bbc.com*, https://www.bbc.com/news/entertainment-arts-57260965.

Kaliss, Jeff. *I Want to Take You Higher: The Life and Times of Sly & the Family Stone*. Backbeat Books, 2008.

Knopper, Steve. *Appetite for Self-Destruction: The Spectacular Crash of the Record Industry in the Digital Age*. Free Press, 2009.

McCartney 3, 2, 1 COMPLETE ! Hulu (2021). *www.youtube.com*, https://www.youtube.com/watch?v=z-b4INqB85I. Accessed 25 Mar. 2023.

Milli Vanilli Have To Give Back Their Grammy - November 19, 1990. https://calendar.songfacts.com/november/19/11065. Accessed 25 Mar. 2023.

O'Brien, Bennett. "Which Video Streaming Service Is Best for Your Budget?" *MoneyGeek.Com*, 30 Mar. 2022, https://www.moneygeek.com/financial-planning/resources/best-streaming-services-on-a-budget/.

Overview of the Fair Labor Standards Act (FLSA). https://www.minimum-wage.org/articles/fair-labor-standards-act. Accessed 15 July 2023.

Philips, Chuck. "HOME ENTERTAINMENT : High Cost of Listening : CDs Rejuvenated Album Sales in the '80s, but Business Is Declining Again and Retailers Say That's Because the Labels Won't Cut Prices." *Los Angeles Times*, 3 May 1992, https://www.latimes.com/archives/la-xpm-1992-05-03-ca-2007-story.html.

Phillips, Helen. "Mind-Altering Media." *New Scientist*, vol. 194, no. 2600, Apr. 2007, pp. 33–37. *DOI.org (Crossref)*, https://doi.org/10.1016/S0262-4079(07)61000-8.

Racoma, Arthur. "80% of Gen Z and Millennials Play Video Games as of 2021." *GamingonPhone*, 9 Aug. 2021, https://gamingonphone.com/news/80-of-gen-z-and-millennials-play-video-games-as-of-2021/.

"Revenue Act of 1964." *Wikipedia*, 22 Jan. 2023. *Wikipedia*, https://en.wikipedia.org/w/index.php?title=Revenue_Act_of_1964&oldid=1135008719.

Ritterhouse, Jennifer Lynn. *Growing up Jim Crow: How Black and White Southern Children Learned Race*. University of North Carolina, 2006.

Saez, Emmanuel, and Gabriel Zucman. "Wealth Inequality in the United States since 1913: Evidence from Capitalized Income Tax Data *." *The Quarterly Journal of Economics*, vol. 131, no. 2, May 2016, pp. 519–78. *DOI.org (Crossref)*, https://doi.org/10.1093/qje/qjw004.

Schmidt, Randy. *Little Girl Blue: The Life of Karen Carpenter*. 1st ed, Chicago Review Press, 2010.

Services, Research. "Two-Thirds of Gen Z Males Say Gaming Is a Core Component of Who They Are." *4A's*, 27 Feb. 2019, https://www.aaaa.org/gen-z-males-say-gaming-core-component-who-they-are/.

Soundcharts | Market Intelligence for the Music Industry. https://soundcharts.com/blog/mechanical-royalties. Accessed 25 Mar. 2023.

"The History of UC Tuition since 1868." *The Daily Californian*, 22 Dec. 2014, https://dailycal.org/2014/12/22/history-uc-tuition-since-1868/.

The Income and Wealth Inequality Crisis in America | U.S. Senate Committee On The Budget. https://www.budget.senate.gov/hearings/the-income-and-wealth-inequality-crisis-in-america. Accessed 25 Mar. 2023.

Vega, Sebastian. "USC Tuition Through the Years." *Daily Trojan*, 6 Mar. 2016, https://dailytrojan.com/2016/03/06/usc-tuition-years/.

Warped Reality | Psychology Today. https://www.psychologytoday.com/us/articles/201609/warped-reality. Accessed 25 Mar. 2023.

"What Happened to California's Free Tuition? A History of Fees and Budget Issues." *Abc10.Com*, https://www.abc10.com/article/news/local/what-happened-to-californias-free-tuition-a-history-of-fees-and-budget-issues/103-465128027. Accessed 25 Mar. 2023.

INDEX

2-track recording, 63–64
4-track recording, 64
8-track recording and tapes, 19, 32, 64
16-track recording, 64–65
24-track recording, 64–65
27 Club, 18
45s (records), 19, 32
1950s, 8–11, 14–15, 63–64
1960s, 16–20, 23, 29, 64
1970s, 21–25, 64–65
1980s, 1–7, 65
1990s, 26–30, 66, 68–69
1996 Telecommunications Act, 26–29, 68–69
2000s, 31–36, 66
2010s, 37–41, 66
2020s, 42–52, 66

active listening, 42–43, 49
African Americans, 8–14, 58
AI (artificial intelligence), 46–48
albums, 31–32, 50–51
Ali, Muhammed, 19
Alpert, Herb, 22
American Idol, 34
"American Pie" (McLean), 16
A&M recording company, 22
Apple iTunes, 31–32, 36, 44, 69
appropriation, 57–59
artificial intelligence (AI), 46–48

Baraka, Amiri, 11–12
The Beatles, 17, 18, 42–43, 64
Bechet, Sidney, 13
Berry, Chuck, 9–10

Bieber, Justin, 44
black artists, 8–14, 58
Blues People (Baraka), 11–12
the Blues, 11–14, 58
Bon Jovi, Jon, 31, 32
Borges, Jorge Luis, 21
bouncing, 64
Brothers, Thomas, 13–14
budget, 67–68. *see also* socioeconomic factors
The Buggles, 26

cable TV, 1, 36, 48
California, 49–52. *see also* socioeconomic factors
capitalism, 28, 69
capitalistic efficiency, 28
The Carpenters, 22
cassette tapes, 19, 24, 32
CDs (Compact Discs), 5–6, 32
cell phones, 34, 35, 37, 48
children. *see* kids/teenagers
choreographed dancing, 4–5
Clark, Gene, 22
Cline, Patsy, 17
Clinton, Bill, 26
Clinton, George, 18

Cobain, Kurt, 29
college expectations, 20, 53–54
college tuition, 33, 41. *see also* socioeconomic factors
Compact Discs (CDs), 5–6
computers, 7, 48
cost of living. *see* socioeconomic factors
costs. *see also* socioeconomic factors
  album production, 22–23
  housing, 48, 49
  music video production, 50–51
  streaming, 48
  video games, 49
Country music, 9
"Crimson and Clover" (Tommy James and the Shondells), 29

dancing, 4–5
Dark Side of the Moon (Pink Floyd), 22–23
Davis, John, 38
Davis, Miles, 59
Dearie, Blossom, 59

digital enhancement, 37–41
digital software plugins, 66
digital streaming. *see* streaming
digital technologies
   in 1980s, 1–2, 5–7, 65
   in 1990s, 66
   enhancement with, 37–41
   influence on pop music, 21–22
disc jockeys (DJs), 43
distraction, 5
DJs (disc jockeys), 27–29, 68–69
doo wop groups, 16

economic conditions. *see* socioeconomic factors
emotional-technical spectrum, 60–61
EPs. *see* records
Epstein, Brian, 17

Farian, Frank, 38
Federal Communications Commission (FCC), 26–27
file sharing, 29, 31
free time, 62–63

Gaye, Marvin, 24
Golden Age of Pop Music, 24, 67
Growing Up Jim Crow (Ritterhouse), 8–9

Harrison, George, 17
Hendrix, Jimi, 18
Holly, Buddy, 16, 58
housing costs, 48, 49. *see also* socioeconomic factors
Houston, Whitney, 4
Howell, Brad, 38

improvisation and solos, 59–60
instrumental music, 59–60
iTunes, 31–32, 36, 44, 69

Jackson, Michael, 2–3
James, Tommy, 29
jazz, 13, 59
Jobs, Steve, 31, 44
Johnson, Robert, 18
Jones, LeRoi. *see* Baraka, Amiri

kids/teenagers
   college expectations, 20, 23–24

and musical
    instruments, 20
and race in 1950s, 8–9
time constraints, 53–54
and video games, 2, 29,
    36, 68

Landis, John, 2–3
layers of perceptive
    elements, 43
Lennon, John, 17
Les Paul guitars, 1970s cost, 24
liner notes, 42–43
Linn drum machine, 65
LPs (Long Play vinyl records),
    5–6, 32

major and minor 3rds, 12–13
Mars, Bruno, 57, 58
Martin, George, 17
McCartney, Paul, 17, 42–43
McLean, Don, 16
Milli Vanilli, 38–41
minor and major 3rds, 12–13
monetization, 32, 42
Morvan, Fabrice, 38–41
MTV (Music Television), 2, 26

music videos
    and appropriation, 59
    costs to produce, 50–51
    as distracting, 5
    MTV, 2
    shift from music to,
        50–51, 59
    Thriller (Jackson), 2–3

nationality, 59
non-prodigies, 54–57

Offering (The Carpenters), 20
orchestras, 35
Osborne, Jeffrey, 4
ownership diversity, 26–27

paradise, 21, 24
personal computers, 7
Phillips, Sam, 10
Pilatus, Rob, 38–41
Pink Floyd, 22–23
pop music, 21–22, 67–69. *see
    also* individual decades
    by name
pop music TV shows, 25
Presley, Elvis, 10–11, 16

prodigies, 54–57
production costs
   albums, 22–23
   music videos, 50–51
program directors, of radio
   stations, 28
Pro Tools, 37, 66
publishing rights, 44–46

race
   and appropriation, 57–59
   and birth of Rock N Roll,
     8–11, 58
   and the Blues, 11–14
radio, 14, 19, 24, 26–29, 60
Rap and Hip-Hop, 29, 36
record companies,
   22–23, 50–51
recording costs, 22–23
recording technology,
   22, 63–66
records, 5–6, 19, 27, 32
Reich, Robert, 33–34
Richardson, J.P., 16
Ritterhouse, Jennifer, 8–9
Rob & Fab, 38–41

Rock N Roll, 8–11, 58, 67
royalties, 31–32, 44

Shaw, Charles, 38
singles, 32
slaves, and the Blues,
   11–14, 58
socioeconomic factors
   1950s, 14–15
   1960s, 18–20, 23
   1970s, 24–25, 32–33
   1980s, 7
   1990s, 29–30
   2000s, 33, 35–36
   2010s, 41
   2020s, 33–34, 48–52
   in the future, 46–47
   historical changes in,
     32–34, 49–52, 70
solos and improvisation, 59–60
space, 28, 47, 51–52,
   63, 67–68
splicing, 65
Spotify, 41
Starr, Ringo, 17
Stills, Stephen, 18

streaming
- costs, 48
- effects on royalties, 44
- influence on pop music, 21–22, 69
- as passive activity, 42, 47, 49
- revenues, 41
- students, 53–54

tapes, 19, 24, 32
tax rates, 70. *see also* socioeconomic factors
technical-emotional spectrum, 60–61
technology. *see also* socioeconomic factors
- AI, 46–48
- cell phones, 34, 35, 37, 48
- digital enhancement, 37–41
- recording technology, 63–66
- transition to digital, 1–2, 5–7, 65–66
- video games, 2, 29, 36, 61–63, 68

teenagers. *see* kids/teenagers
Telecommunications Act of 1996, 26–29
television. *see* TV (television)

Thriller (Jackson), 2–3
ticket prices, 3–4
time constraints, 43–44, 53–54, 62–63, 67–68
Tommy James and the Shondells, 29
Tower Records, 5
TV (television)
- in 1950s, 14
- in 1960s, 19
- in 1970s, 24–25
- and 1996 Telecommunications Act, 26
- cable, 1, 36, 48

Valens, Richie, 16
Van Halen, Eddie, 18
video games, 2, 29, 36, 49, 61–63, 68
"Video Killed the Radio Star" (The Buggles), 26
videos. *see* music videos
vinyl promo pressings, 27
virtuosity, 60
visual media. *see* music videos

wages, 33–34, 49

www.ingramcontent.com/pod-product-compliance
Lightning Source LLC
Chambersburg PA
CBHW032057150426
43194CB00006B/553